THE NEIGHBORHOOD YEARS

This Book Belongs To

Bottom Dog Press
Working Lives Series

THE NEIGHBORHOOD YEARS

David Kherdian

Introduction by David Shevin

Working Lives Series
Bottom Dog Press
Huron, Ohio

Bottom Dog Press
c/o BGSU Firelands College
Huron, Ohio 44839
lsmithdog@aol.com

Cover & Book Design
Nonny Hogrogian

We wish to thank The Ohio Arts Council
for its continuing support
of our publishing program.

The Ohio Arts Council helped fund
this organization with state tax dollars
to encourage economic growth,
educational excellence and cultural
enrichment for all Ohioans.

CONTENTS

A man with Mediterranean features and a Nietzche moustache leans forward in his seated position, hands fingering prayer beads against his knee. He wears an expression of deep contemplation. Beside him on the ground, a boy draws his knees up. The child is physically close to the man, but his gaze turns in another direction altogether. His hand is to his eyes, and a smile of wonder and exploration shines on his face. This is the cover of HOMAGE TO ADANA, the book of poems David Kherdian gifted me with in 1976.

This early book took its title from his father Melkon's hometown, now a part of Turkey, and set up a mythology about the Armenian immigrant community in Racine, Wisconsin. The book was sent from William Saroyan's town of Fresno, and shared Saroyan's vision of joy in adversity, and triumph of the uncommon common people. Saroyan, in fact, speaks the book's epigraph, which says: "No art deserves to be above the life of its time. No living people deserve to be beneath the art of their time. If there is to be dancing, it must at least be what the living dreamed." The influence is real, and the disciple was mapping a territory to be explored in many powerful, varied and affecting subsequent volumes. I loved that early book. I would take it with me to my poets-in-the-schools assignments, and share tales with the little ones about the Greek Popcorn Man and the defiant United States Tony, and the pool-shooting State Street Harry. I invited them to mythologize themselves with nicknames and exotic character traits, to use the poetry as their own boasting and inventing space.

In this world of industry and shipping, the Armenian coffee house, the smells of youth, the father is memorialized and remembered. Here, too, Kherdian was finding his material for the Root River Cycle of eleven volumes, material drawn from and feeding back to the experience of his city, his family, and his culture. The material recol-

1

lects and reflects with the very best of American immigrant experience. The books will alternately speak of friends and relatives, will speak to the river and place, and to history. The poems of CHIPPECOT-TON create a community history of Racine full of the personality and mesh of culture that invent a place. The book gobbles the soil of the lakeshore with the same kind of verve and vision William Carlos Williams brought to Patterson.

This book is part of the public and personal picture of Root River Kherdian has created. Sometimes the city comes to life through individualized experience, sometimes through the family, the friends, and the extended family. There is also through all of the Root River books a love of the cultures meeting as the meld of personalities pitches itself into a fellowship, the kind of place that delivers anonymous Christmas gifts after a father's crippling accident and transplants the heroes of Ararat into Wisconsin myths. Through these chronicles, the personalities of the early book would reappear, become more varied, full and familiar.

There is an education throughout these tales of the peculiar autonomy, springing to and from the independent struggles and sacrifices of 1918-21, that the Armenian immigrant community carries. In the personalities, despair meets refusal of desperation, kindness prevails stubbornly over the misanthropy of history.

The boy on the cover of the early book? The final poem announced that he would "have to follow / these factory spilled / waters beyond the city / limits." This was the circumstance given "if he was ever to keep / his boyhood and his / manhood and his children / alive." The tale echoes Sherwood Anderson departing Clyde for Chicago. It foreshadows, too, Kherdian's journey of books, explorations, and moves. I don't know many writers with such accumulated and fluid wisdom as he brings to the many topics of his work.

His career as historian, memoirist, and editor naturally led him to the publication of *Forkroads*. The magazine was an act of inclusiveness and generosity. As a "Journal of Ethnic American Literature," the magazine reflected the view of society in the hometown books. The picture was specifically celebratory, an open door for writers to claim the exoticism and the mystery of their rootedness.

Comes now the eleventh book of the Root River Cycle.

THE NEIGHBORHOOD YEARS embraces "our home and residence, / our habitation and name" with a generosity suggested decades ago and now fulfilled. Here again are, as Kherdian presents them, "the people whose poems / became my life;" they are the watchmen and the cooks and the shopkeepers of memory, all so human and varied and alive in a rich and poignant fabric.

The method this writer has developed to tell his stories is to engage us at once in the teller's and the subject's experience. Adventuring, for example, with childhood friend Howie Sell, the narrator allows the adolescents to act as adolescents among the hidden secrets of the back streets. The movement toward sexuality and experience is described as the distances reached in bike time, "that / teen time, when the invisible clock was ticking / inside our loins." This is precision.

They come alive, these people of Chippecotton (the Miami Indian word for Root River), from haunted Mrs. Giragosian to Kookoolala, to the rag and paper man and old Mr. Buchaklian. They live in their nuances, their claims on memory, and a dearness that transcends nostalgia to document a place that is triumphant over its own driven pasts, economic struggles, spiritual crises, and dramas. Finally, the Racine of this book is a place of blessing.

That blessing is hard won. The challenges of parents and workers recognize the realities of class and limited reward to many of the society. The shift worker carries his cold recognition that punching the clock means that "the eagle shits on Friday," and the Ace Grill may have to close down. Such real recognition never slows the connections from discoveries to celebrations to love through the entire neighborhood. In addition to Saroyan, the flavor of these tales recollects the poignancy of the New York of Michael Gold. In JEWS WITHOUT MONEY, the publishing sensation of 1930, Gold described at once an East Side that could become the joyous circus of a summer where everything happens at once, and then turn around to ask, "Why is there so much gloomy wisdom at the hearts of the poor? " (283)

Here, too, in these Armenian cafes, side streets and wondrous personalities, Kherdian documents wisdom, reflected over great distances since that boy sat at the feet of the bead-holder. For this, we can be grateful for a such a rich book, such a vision. Thank you, David.

David Shevin
Tiffin, Ohio / July, 2000

WORKS CITED:

Gold, Michael. JEWS WITHOUT MONEY. New York: Carroll & Graf, 1984.

Kherdian, David. CHIPPECOTTON: ROOT RIVER TALES OF RACINE. Sebastopol, CA: Gatehouse, 1998.

Kherdian, David. HOMAGE TO ADANA. Fresno: The Giligia Press, 1971. (unpaginated)

THE NEIGHBORHOOD YEARS

To

JOE PERCH

DEDE

STATE STREET HARRY

BILL MILLER

KOOKOOLALA

RUBY

UMBAJI

UNITED STATES TONY

WILLIE

BILL ZAEHLER

Whether mad, eccentric, retarded, unmoored, adrift,
or simply characters on a mission to fortune and mercy,
they followed their stars over one lifetime
and helped point me toward mine

MONUMENT SQUARE

The favorite corner of one's hometown
appears often in memory, when with eyes
closed, we are reminded of what was given,
where we came from and what we are—

Main and Sixth, which included the entire extent
of Monument Square, the twin pooled land-
scaped statued park, that became
our city's signature—

With its many offices and buildings, surrounding:
The Postal Telegraph Office, Brown's Bookstore,
Fanny Farmer's, and the once grand Hotel Racine,
as well as the Post Office just across from there—

And that became the view, mostly aerial,
that I would carry in my mind's eye
until it became the emblem
of what I called Home—

And some part of the ghostly hearts
of all those who passed are collected there;
the gathered body keeping the living soul
of that city alive.

OUR TOWN

It isn't the isolated city
    we remember so much
    as we do the locales—
    the many places where we
    put our mark

Feeling the fingertips
    of mortal time
    shared by those
    whose passages paralleled our own
    as well as those who
    preceded us in time

Next to the ramshackle
    building that housed the
    Armenian coffee house beside
    Rognerud's filling station—
    an American place—

Across the street from
    Slippery Corners Tavern
    (that I would never enter)
    beside Derse's Drug Store,
    where I was often found—
    or lost—pouring over the
    latest comics
    or staring out its plate glass
    windows and door
    at the traffic beyond

The buildings as much a part
   of our lives as the people
   who inhabited them,
   the strangers on the street
   as essential to our lives
   as those we called friend,
   all of it a part of that place:
   our home and residence,
   our habitation and name

THE LAKE

We had a lake to walk to
   to look out upon
To go to alone
   or with others
bathing trunks
   wrapped in a towel
in one hand
   inner tube in the other
the sun just rising
   or in full glory overhead

or with poles in hand
   keeping to father's step
or alone on our bikes
   looking out from
the circular pavilion—
   the sloping lawn
meeting sand
   at the water's edge

Later in cars—
   and always, going
north or south,
   we followed the lake—
our talisman
   the beacon from
our lighthouse
   visible from shore

Sand and bathers
   picnickers
with lunch baskets
   sitting above
on the grass
   with games of catch,
relatives and friends

When the perch ran
   the poles danced—
for smelt we dipped with nets—
   minnows we seined—

Friday Nite Fish Fry
   all over town
the lake darkly distant
   humming in our ears
and each time the door opened
   the elemental night reappeared

MARBLES

for Khatchik "Lotch" Oglanian

Of all the games, was marbles the best?
The form we devised, outside the traditional
form—that was never popular with any of us—
though some did draw a circle, and taking turns,
tried to knock the smaller marbles
out of the ring with the large Shooter—
and while it seemed a good enough idea,
that we even saw advertised in pictures
drawn by Norman Rockwell—
nevertheless our way, which included travel,
risk, absurd luck, charm (as in *divine* luck),
played itself out inside the ritual
of chasing one marble after another
down the block, or across the lot,
until a hit was made
and the marble changed hands.

At the very least, we played our way home
from school with long shots, and short shots,
and with our marbles sometimes squashed
or squirted out of sight by passing automobiles,
or rolling down embankments, into sewers,
or dangerously close to Kookoolala's hovel—
and all the other out-of-bounds territories
where the marbles might be lost—
as we scrambled and scuffled and bragged,
hooting triumph and squealing defeat
up and down those streets

coded in memory and blood
that were simply the routes
leading from home to school
and then back again.

THE SONG

The rag man calling from
his horse-drawn wagon

the tingling bell
of the ice-cream man

the sharp pincers on ice
heaved over burlapped shoulders

of the grunting ice-men
coming up stairs

the bicycle-propelled
scissor and knife-sharpening man

there on the sidewalk of
our summery home

the blacksmith on the
block below hammering

his black apron
deflecting orange sparks

the reverberating sounds
in the city that once embodied me

the people whose poems
became my life

THE MILK MAN

I remember him best as the father
of my childhood friend
in large striped suspendered trousers,
mounting his milk truck
from the back, hoisting
bottles of milk with his large
rough hands

placing them carefully
on the doorsteps
brown or white milk
through thick clear glass,
cream rising in one, the other
pure chocolate brown
with the name on the bottle
I knew to be his

SUPERIOR STREET
for Sam Margosian

We were perhaps lucky that it was no
    longer a going factory
there across the street from
    our house, where we stood
throwing stones at the few
    remaining windows that hadn't
yet been broken

The city hadn't paved the street
    to that point
where we played pick-up
    ball games—two or three
to a side
    in the dirt and dust of
our dead end block

Raising the noise level to a pitch
    that still could not have matched
what must have once come
    from that factory
but loud enough for the neighbors
    certainly
though they never complained
    in those easy days
of our modest lives.

THE BLACKSMITH SHOP
for Jerry Hansen

The blacksmith shop was below
our dead end street, that T'd
at Prospect, where the
blacksmith shop stood

recessed, seemingly designed
to best display the works
it freely scattered in front
on its cement lawn

catching the attention
of the passer-by
in particular the children
on those blocks

the taciturn, black-aproned
blacksmith inside, or
at the door, watching
the street with thoughts

different from ours, imagining
uses for the things he made
in clamor and soot

the fire inside, the black-
ness and orange flame
from which his creations
would slowly appear
before our eyes

PLACES IN THE HEART

Prominent still in the mind's eye was the
J. I. Case Main Office on State, corner
of Douglas Avenue. Its austere brick structure
obliged us to acknowledge it—but always
in our own way—each time we passed.

On Sundays, when it was unoccupied, we'd walk
the first story ledge for the fun it allowed,
always on the way home from the movies,
and it was on that corner, where Ardie would
split off from me and Mikey on his way home,
that he let us in on the identity of the masked
man, called The Lone Ranger,
which seemed so amazing at the time,
and it was on that corner again that I first
saw my father marching in a parade, behind the
VFW flag, where I knew he belonged.

That corner and building were but two of the places
I knew, that were altogether a mysterious
part of my unknowable life, as I attempted
to unravel the inner workings that were bound
by outer conditions, that seemed to contain
my days, attempting to see myself in the world
and to see how the world fitted inside of me.
The multiple threads I was using,
that all of us were using,
to weave the growing designs of our lives.

BILLBOARDS
for Mikey Kaiserlian

There at street level between
the Mainstreet Theatre and
the building it nearly adjoined
was a large very large billboard
that advertised the coming events—
the B Westerns and Gangster movies
we seemingly could not live without.

You could look through the wooden
lattice work at its base to the empty
lot below while waiting, the Saturday
matinee lines extending all the way
to there, and sometimes as far
as the State Street bridge,
another fifty yards beyond.

We never tired of the larger than life
images whose living presences would
soon be reflected on the silver screen
in the coming week, making us just as
anxious over the movies we hoped
to see as those we were about to watch.

POLES

Whatever else the State Street Hardware store
    was notable for
        what comes easily to mind
Was the tubular holder out front—
    there on the sidewalk—
        that held all of the store's cane poles
Just waiting for prospective fishermen
    to test them against the open air—
        the sky substituting for the water's blue—

That we could freely approach whenever we liked
    to test the whip and snap
        and to sight with cocked head
And opened eye, its straightness & length
    before imagining the perch
        on the end of the line—
Testing its suppleness, the weight it might hold,
    while measuring by feel
        its breaking point

It was there that my emerging wanderings
    took hold, that I followed
        to the lake's pier & shore
Where I would go with my father
    as soon as he said I was
        old enough—
He with a bucket for the fish we'd catch
    and of course
        our lunch

And me with a bucket of crabs
      caught under the Island
            Park bridge
With each a cane pole of our own
      that I had picked out
            with my father's help
On the State Street Hardware walk

THE COFFEE HOUSE
for Naz Gengozian

It seemed fitting that it
was unpainted, unwashed,
uncared for and neglected
and therefore a perfect haunt
for the Armenians from
the other side

A coffee house, or *sourjarran*,
in the old country language
from where they
had lately come

Inside that singular space
beyond what the name foretold
was something more than
backgammon board & dice

There, outside the fenced-in
enclosure of Garfield School,
with us too frightened
to ever enter inside

Our curiosity sated by
the stolen glance, the
furtive look into that large
smoke-filled room

The inhabitants dressed
in grays and browns
somber, silent, belonging
to a world outside of ours

That was somehow also ours
for these were our fathers,
the other half
of the split-off world

We knew only as Armenia,
a name and a tragedy
they could revisit, but that we
dared not enter with our lives

RICE
for Ralph Molbeck

There was BR time and AR time in our
young lives, although of course we never
expressed it in this way. That is, Rice's
Bicycle Shop Before, and then, Rice's
Bicycle Shop After. BR meant looking
in the window, or bravely entering
and pretending to want to buy a bike,
when everyone knew, especially Mr. Rice,
that you could not do so until your
father said you were ready for one.

But Old Man Rice would greet us from
his place in back, where he made his repairs.
He never pushed us, or asked questions.
Instead he waited to answer ours.
This went on for years. The great
bicycle-dreaming time of our lives.
Then in the AR, when I finally got my Red Racer,
we would go in for accessories, for patches
to fix our flats, or to look at the latest designs,
and just to brag and chat.

No conveyance, not the wagon or the
tricycle that preceded that bike, nor
the cars that followed—the trains and
planes and ships that carried me across
the land and over the world—meant
as much as that bike did. Nor did any

station depot, terminal, or dock ever
again hold the magic of that wooden-floored,
special rubber-grease-metal odor
of Rice's Bicycle Shop, there on State
Street, around the corner from Marquette,
whether in our AR or BR mode,
it was always there in living time.

BYWAYS

for Howie Sell

We avoided the neighborhood streets
whenever we could,
preferring the byways and pathways—
those ways of getting from one place
to another that we found on our own,
the routes we took that adults seldom traversed,
or had the imagination for,
nor the foolish daring to try.

Sometimes, in the middle of a block,
there might be a narrow opening between
a building or garage, that we could slip through
sideways—that saved going up one block
and then down, thus preserving precious time.

But that was not really the point,
because of course we had time for everything.
It was what our imaginations evoked
taking the shortcut, whether alone or with
another, pretending to be a character from
one of the running serials at the Badger
or Rialto, or a character in one of the
hightone dramas at the Venetian Theater.

Between the last house on our block and
the rear of the building that belonged to State,
there was a dividing board in back,
between that building and an empty lot,

that we slipped over sideways,
first with the right leg, then with the left,
leading us to the rear door of the Kummel Bakery,
where custard was left out to cool overnight,
that we snuck up on till they got wise.

And so it went, all those years even before we were
old enough for bikes, which then led us to explore
the outer reaches of our neighborhood,
and other neighborhoods, and also the town,
traveling out to girls, delving into secrets we were
sometimes prepared for and sometimes not,
but always eager to reach in bike-time—that
teen-time, when the invisible clock was ticking
inside our loins.

PIEL

The Piels were known for living among us
but in a different world.
Their house, a simple white clapboard
in the middle of our block,
was yet a castle of awnings and colored trim—

With an ornament, even, over his garage.
A flagpole rose up from his manicured lawn,
but with a treeless backyard,
not a fruit tree or vegetable growing anywhere,
unlike the rest of us—

And they had no children, either,
which is maybe also why he
frightened us: knowing
we did not trust him;
nor could he trust us
and so he left nothing
lying around
that our eyes might rest upon—

His off-limits lawn fit only
for a patriotic flag,
telling us how the nation
mourned or prayed,
occasions
it was unlikely
had anything to do with the rest of us.

THE FIRE ESCAPE
for Jack Povkovich

It was there, outside the 6th grade
second story window,
where my imagination took hold
and made its stand against
everything I was being taught
in those classrooms and deadly

Corridors, the stuffy cloakrooms
where we remained imprisoned
when punished, and it was
rotten awful, all of it

But for the fire escape chute
whose entrance was at the back
of our classroom that final year,
though used only sparingly for drills,
never once for real

Then upon reaching the glorious
end of our swift-ending ride
we'd be marched back upstairs,
but for the rare times it became
the last event of the day

When we would bounce onto the earth
and run screaming through the yard
thrilled to be released from our holding cells
in the only way that ever seemed fitting and right.

STATIONS

for Ray Rodriguez

The two watch guard stations
on the State Street Bridge
were simply there, inhabited
by invisible watchmen,
who of course knew when
and how to raise the bridge
for the waterway traffic,
and then how to lower it
once the boats had passed.

For them, the rolling gears of
machinery, and for us the physical
presence of a bridge making miracles,
enlarging our idea of space and time
while we studied those brooding archways
that watched over the waters beneath
connecting us to the life of that place
and all life beyond.

KOOKOOLALA

Eli had gone crazy we thought
and called him such

watching him pull his wagon
filling an empty house

that none would enter
certainly not us

M

Was he the only Armenian drunk
or only the one most visible
and known to us

whose family lived just a few
blocks away, with a son who
was strange and shy and always ill at ease

who later became an artist,
later still the owner of a tackle shop,
like me a fishermen all his life

who I never saw again, because
like his father—who had long since
disappeared into that waiting place—

he too disappeared, but by his own hand
with no one to explain what had happened
or why, but only to tell me what I already knew

that he was the second to suicide
from among those I grew up with
in the streets & alleys & waterways
of our town

YELLOW BRICKS
for Dick Steberl

There was no iron oxide in the
thin vein of purplish clay
running through the city's north side,
and so, when it was dried and kiln-fired,
it turned a pale yellow, or cream color,
instead of an expected red—

But we didn't know this then
nor did we think our bricks
unusual, or even unique
of this place—
staring up at that yellow brick chimney
across from our house
that seemed so special to me then,
traveling straight up, higher than
any house or nearby building,
serving that factory it stood beside—

And the sparrows that lived
there, flying in and out of those apertures
near the top,
were not unique of course
except to us—
because they moved among us,
as members of our tribe,
pecking on the sidewalk
or on our tiny patch of grass—

Beings of the air and ground,
with a dual existence to our one,
scrambling and scrounging
like us, and like us, here and gone—

Except they could leave by wing,
suddenly, and seated atop their chimney
look down at us—
ordinary citizens dazed with life.

NEXT DOOR

The house next door
was not ten feet away
with its second story
porch directly across
from our side door entrance
where the Peterson's
lived, son Glenny
my sort-of-friend
who sometimes talked with me
from there
but I don't remember
ever being invited up
like his cousins were
with whom I also
conversed
while standing on
the cement stoop
below, outside
our rear door,
and some part of me
is there still
looking up, waiting
to speak—
having just been
spoken to
by Donny Hansen,
his cousin,
my other neighbor
and kind-of-friend

HEROES
for Willie

Take the men one by one
shadows, influences, reminders
of what but the self:
unrecognized,
          unknown

Searching, as that one did
with his wagon, alive,
smiling his retarded smile into
          the bright sun

Against the streets where we found him
going and coming,
away from the busy traffic, yet within
          our own

His moment of truth
forever inside us, his wagon trailing
          behind

C M

He stood inside the windowed door
of his tavern on Douglas Avenue
on that stark block
of factories and businesses
that served workers, stragglers, the down
and out—

Waiting for the first passerby
in the early
morning light
when the call of sea gulls
the distant fog horn
were the only sound—

Knocking on the window
with his knuckles
motioning the stranger
to come inside
so his first drink of the day
would not be taken alone and apart.

MADAME G
for Clara Sahagian

Long before the Giragosian Grocery Store
became an island of wonder for me
it had been a place of importance
for my mother and father as well,
and not just a place where they shopped.
As the city grew and changed
markets flourished
and other meeting places began to appear
until the importance of Giragosian's Grocery Store
began to diminish in their lives.

But not for me or my friends.
For apart from the ice cream man
theirs was the place of sweets,
from twinkies to candy bars,
and most importantly, penny candy,
but also for games of chance—that led
to the purchasing of even more goodies
or prizes when we won.

It was also at Giragosian's that we studied
the new fangled machine that sliced meat,
while we took in the odors
that were similar to the odors of our homes,
with their machine providing cold cuts, as well.
Mrs. Giragosian, the bossy owner
had been a forerunner in the diaspora,

my mother turning to her for advice
and remedies when I was sick as a boy;
and then as I grew, her disciplinary
tongue kept me in line.
I entered there casually, with caution,
prepared for the particulars of memory
and also the sudden surprise
for I took my education that way
and in the streets
with that store the midway point
between the cultures of school and home.

STOLEN

Even then bicycles were stolen
stripped and thrown
into the river.
I know because of the
one found by Ron Gardina.

Seeing it was a Schwinn
and red, he delivered it
to my home, believing
it must be my lost bike.

And soon we were riding
to town again,
with new tires, handlebars,
pedals, and all the rest—
because it was the frame alone
he had brought to my door.

BUDDIES

for John "Bud" Graham

The street lights went on overhead
joining us to the games the night
was calling us to,
followed by secret confabs
on the curb
before illicit cigarette
smoking occurred
behind the boarded-up
red fence
belonging to the factory
below our block

And the raiding of gardens
including our parents' own
the bonfires at night
where we baked our
stolen spuds,
Butsy and Bill
on their harmonicas
we at their side

Among the lost backyards
of America
with a fallen moon
the only light

COOK

for George Kamakian

Cook's Bait Shack was one of a kind
there at the entrance of the pier,
below Barker Street, and perched
on the sand, not fifty yards from
the lapping waters of Lake Michigan.

In size only five feet by ten, if that,
but inside those precious feet of space
Old Man Cook sold live minnows
and occasionally crabs, with potato chips,
candy bars, cold sodas, and of course fishing
gear: lines, sinkers & hooks, as well
as bells & weights, and whatever else
the unimaginative trolling fishermen needed,
and also fully rigged cane poles for a dollar deposit
against the ten cent fee per pole.

He worked the shack himself, but he had
kids working for him as well,
going up and down the pier, selling candy
bars and soda, as well as bait, and I'm sure
they kept Old Man Cook apprised of the
situation, so he could keep his supplies
up to snuff, though there didn't seem to be
room for reserves of any kind.

No matter what, before entering the pier,
we checked in with Old Man Cook.
It was like having our tickets punched.
And, too, we preferred to give him our business
before anyone else, knowing he would
always be there, with comments
on the weather, the best means of fishing,
and which baits were best on any given day;
or if the fish were biting, and if not, his
prediction of when they would start.

THE HOME

Each evening the same—mother
in the kitchen, finishing up
the work of one day while
preparing for the next,
with father on the couch in his
BVDS, work pants & slippers,
smoking, his lips moving over the
Armenian newspaper, and myself
before the radio waiting for Jack
Armstrong to come on the air.

The living room was reserved
for company, where we kept the
best of everything we had, and it
stayed that way because it was *meant*
to stay that way: new, showy,
the best we had to offer, but only
for company, which we needed for
some reason to impress.

In the basement, I rigged up a hoop
for shooting baskets with a rubber
ball, near where Mother did the wash
and Father stoked the coal furnace,
there beside the coal bin, beside the pantry
where we kept our preserves.

And this is how we lived and passed
our days, each of us attendant to the
hour, that for me was the ongoing present,
because I had no time past to blur
the time ahead, unlike my parents
who were attempting to make new rituals
out of a broken ritual I knew nothing about.

HORLICK'S ATHLETIC FIELD
for Ulysses Doss

Our most famous athletic field—
if famous it was—was, like our high school,
named after the Horlicks,
whose plant made the malted milk tablets
that *were* famous
or at least known to the world outside—

unlike Horlick Athletic Field
that was famous only to us
because Jackie Robinson once played there
before he reached the majors
and hit a home run, thrilling the fans forever,
an event that became a permanent part
of our tenuous myth and lore—

but if I missed that event (being too young)—
and much of the talk that followed—
I didn't miss the Racine Belles, of the
All-Girls Professional Baseball League
with their short-skirted canary yellow uniforms
beneath the baseball caps
they bobby-pinned into place—

thrilling us and distracting us from
the concerns of the war
because for us they were more
than just a distraction, or morale booster,
they were *ours* and belonged to *us,*

and when I looked out from the stands
there—as irreplaceable as the sun,
and as golden, stood Clara Schillace,
the pig-tailed, olive-skinned centerfielder
with whom I was in love, and with whom
I stayed in love all the years
they played on that field,
when I was youth-wounded
and the world unstrung.

A & W / WEST AT STATE
for Harold "Bobby" Vakos

We plunked down our nickels & dimes
while standing in the evening air
strangely alert, under evening lights,
on the brink of some great adventure

sensing girls—who were not yet
there—drinking our root beer
and eating our mustard & ketchup dogs

at the end of the world on the outskirts
of our neighborhood,
our lives itching for something

true & honorable & right

PARKS AND THE RIVER

The parks gave us what nothing
else could provide:
The anticipation of fireworks
at Washington Park
there upon the golf course lawn,
the streets winding around
the river park, dissecting
the bordering bridges
before that river curled back on itself
then flowed onward to that
other park called Lincoln
that I can look back on now
from above, as if the city
had been made from there

While I enter solemnly the kingdom
of lawns and trees & moving water
beside leaves of grass,
and those brick-lined passageways
over which my feet first roamed—
that shielded arbor between sloping hill
and river, dipping down and up
with our bikes following the same paths
we first walked with cane poles in hand,
and again the same weaving bodies
of T-shirted boys, with trunks
under their pants, or yet bare-
bottomed, diving off the trees
that swooned over those mud-
brown banks

ACE GRILL

I would not have believed that one day our
very own Ace Grill would close down.
It had, we felt, permanently preserved
itself by making a special niche inside
our minds, where I can picture it still
in my own, as I can feel its existence yet
within my body and inside my heart.

Located on Main Street, next to the Venetian
Theater, it had a winding counter, with booths
against one wall, where adults took their
coffee—in those days usually with pie—if they
weren't there for sandwiches or a hot lunch.

We were not old enough for that. Instead
we went to the one place we did belong,
the pool hall downstairs, its descending entrance
across from the cash register counter,
and just shy of the booths.

As we sauntered nonchalantly toward the stairs,
we took in the ambience of the place,
adult and worldly, making us feel self-conscious
and out of place because of our inexperience and age.
We'd quickly disappear down the cellar stairs

Into the dark, smoke-filled chamber of green
felt tables, each lit by a green-shaded bulb,
and with Sarge at the counter, giving out balls and

racking the games, before collecting the loser's
dime. Serious, glum, stern, unsmiling, with
jowls like an English mastiff, he was the
acknowledged icon of that dungeon, and as self-
created, as permanent and irreplaceable,
as we were fleeting—like water bugs skating
before a huge unyielding boulder placed
at the entrance of that pond.

And that is why, when I heard from a distance
that it had closed down, it was as if an entity
had died; not something with mortal bearing,
but rather a being, imperishable, an embodiment
of an unnamed tradition, whose history was us—
our mortal time that begged for consecration
and permanence in some form, that we could
turn to when attempting to name our lives.

FERRIER'S

for Angie Alaimo and Janet Bilik

There are some places that
are remembered even when

nothing that happened there
can be recalled. Which means

only that it was a regular
place, as we were the

ordinary inhabitants
within those walls—

especially on Friday nights
after the Douglas Park dance

when our feet went from
skimming pine floors

to shuffling up the long
cement walk, to meet,

to mingle, to flirt—and to
drink a malted or milk shake

before walking our current
girlfriend home

STATE STREET
for Dolly Fredericksen

It was the Dane's town
      before we moved there
            and they left for the far West Side
And so it was not surprising that the Danish stores
        outnumbered those of the Armenians
           causing a blending of the once familiar
with the suddenly strange—
      the storeroom odors new
          in each of the different stores
open burlap sacks that were ever present
      at the Boranian Grocery Store
         but less visible at Christensen's
where the unpackaged goods were stored in back.

If this is how *we* were becoming Americanized,
      were the Danes being Americanized as well?
        Or had they already been—
or did they just look American,
      as we believed we did not.
        Nor did we believe that this slow acquainting
of people & place & foods & smells,
      along with the varied look of all of us,
        the miscellaneous languages we spoke,
with varied dialects and accents,
      was making us all, over time, into Americans
        because of—not in spite of—
all our various commingling parts.

ITINERANTS

for Even "Junior" Rognerud

What of the stores that weren't
stationary, the services that
moved by foot & pedal & wagon.
Or pulled by man, or that were horse-
drawn. Also the pick-up truck.

Weren't these the businesses
closest to our hearts.
Because in our minds they
were not businesses at all
or even enterprises
but something quite other
that we couldn't quite define
except to give them the name
they were represented by—

Mr. Miller, the radio repairman,
who smoked a cigar as no one else
could, who came to our door
with his satchel of tools—

The rag & paper man on his
horse-drawn wagon,
his clipped, accented speech
flitting the air

The stranger on bicycle
with a contraption for sharpening
scissors and knives—
the painter who gave us his life history
and for no extra charge—Mr. File.

And best of all the bicycle-propelled
ice cream wagon man with his musical bell
that our sharp ears were attuned to hear
from far blocks away.

And we felt—without needing to
make our claim—
that this was the way to do business
and the only way to be alive—
not realizing that these men were
at the low end of the totem pole
of economics, without power or prestige,
except for their influence over us,
feeding our souls ahead of our bodies.

And so I went on studying them from
my armchair in the streets
which was the seat of my pants
by which I sailed through my coming years
negotiating all my God-given rights
over the tenure of that block.

MEIER

for Chuck "Horse" Kamakian

We often went to Meier's Sports Shop
peering in the window when there
was nothing we could afford to buy

and maybe that's why he sponsored
our softball team, comprised of us
neighborhood kids who played in

the sandlots of the city league.
I was proud of that uniform
which consisted simply of a sweatshirt

and a cap, and looked forward
always to donning my outfit
for the weekly Saturday game

until later when we played under the lights
as life grew less tame and safe and quiet
as we blustered our way onto

the city scene, trying to make our mark
and put our name up there
in lights, that we imagined

existed somewhere, even for us,
thinking we knew where such
ambitions led, or what they might

mean for us, and also for their influence
over our friends, which was our
world then and our life

THE CRAB & MINNOW BAIT GARAGES
for Bill Zaehler, Jr.

This was my idea of what a business
should be and could be if it was run
by someone who was in possession

of his life. For once, such a garage had
been ours, but it was so worn, lopsided
and dilapidated that it wasn't good

for anything, but maybe Father's
gardening tools, and so Mother rented
it to our neighbor, Bill Zaehler, for fifty

cents a month. He put in minnow
tanks and large buckets for crabs and
nightcrawlers, with a contraption

that kept the water moving, creating
oxygen for the living minnows
he sold for a quarter a dozen, though

I don't recall ever seeing a customer
cough up any such coin, or even make
an entrance into that holy shrine

where I hung out whenever I could
along with Bill's nephews, who were
my buddies and his helpmates, and so

all in all it looked to me like the greatest
American enterprise imaginable, with
a future as bright and as certain as was

the sorrow that brooded on our side
of the fence, where we were housing the
past, while inching towards our own

New America, over which my imagination
wandered, my eyes on the nets poled out
for drying in their yard, their dog Bozo

keeping me at bay, sensing my foreignness
and my fear, my inability to insinuate myself
into the easy ways of his master and his

cohorts—those casual designers of milieus
and dramas American; vast unending
panoramas of casual sense

THE CHINESE LAUNDRY
for Julie Der Garabedian

Was it important only because
        it stood there alone
                an unpainted clapboard

Isolated on the
        opposite side
                of the street

From the other businesses
        on that block
                that were stuck brick to brick

Or was it the tradition
        of the Chinese laundry
                as American landmark

To be separate
        and distinct
                a thing apart

A tradition onto itself
        part of the American
                colloquialism:

"No ticky, no laundry"
        lodged
                inside our heads

Repeating itself involuntarily
      each time we passed
            that odd storefront building

The family alone
      behind curtains
            somewhere upstairs

Or was it the unsmiling presence
      of the one who came
            to the counter there

Never answering our spoken words
      with more than
            a brief utterance of his own

Or was it that they were *us*
      and we *them*,
            taking us years

to unravel
      the truth, the simple truth,
            of our neighborhood lives

U. S. OF A.

for Marilyn Witkofski

When the Case whistle went off
in the '40s, it wasn't just men who
came rushing out of the factory
gates, but women, too, moving slowly,
proudly, not like us in a rush—

But also heading home, and if it was odd
to see them in jeans, their hair tied up
in a bandanna, it was natural, also,
the war effort bringing us together in a way
we had not been brought together before,
stamps and coupons, war bonds and rationing,
our pride in a war effort we called our own

While we watched it all from under
the visors of our caps, trading baseball cards
for war cards—our heroes of old
now suspended for these heroes
of new—Colin Kelly, Jr., bomber
pilot, my favorite—but all of them
going up—not in smoke
but to the tune of new songs
in harmony with the aromatic saliva-producing
gum inside our cards, as well as
any artifacts of war we could find
making souvenirs and prizes
things to collect and cherish
making us Americans as we had not been before.

OH OLFACTORY
for Sam Balian

I liked that we lived in a smelly town.
Which is to say, I like it now, in full
awareness that I did not think to
like it then, complaining in chorus
with the others over the odors
that arose from the tannery
on Sixth Street, beside the bridge
over Root River, that I wasn't even aware it
was contaminating then—

Its assault on those waters more damaging
than the effect of its toxins upon my nose;
those and the odors of the Wink Soap
factory on West Street,
that I passed most of the days of my life—

For how would it have been to live in a place
that didn't smell, that couldn't distinguish itself
with odors that were malodorous, offensive,
or even surprisingly delightful—as no factory
or foundry smell ever was of course—

Except to the "remembered nose" that wishes to
follow itself back to those days, once encapsulated
by industry and its own designs, as I was once
encapsulated within my own imagination, swaying
with my companions down those awful unforgettable streets
that were ours, when that place was our only home.

TAVERNS

for Ardie Kaiserlian

I didn't at first question the taverns
        the great number of them,
                or the goings on inside.
All I knew was that we had more of them
        than all the movie houses,
                filling stations, drug stores
and hardware stores combined,
        and you could throw in both depots,
                and whatever post office buildings
we had at the time, and still the number
        would not equal the taverns alone that stood
                on State Street and Douglas Avenue.

And it didn't stop there, for they were sprawled out
        all over town,
                serving neighborhoods, business
districts, the factories where the men worked,
        or those near the banks because
        saloon keepers also cashed the workers' checks.

When Friday night rolled around
        and the eagle perched atop
                J. I. Case's factory performed
on its local payday expression:
        "The eagle shits on Friday "
                when the taverns would be full, the laughter
and shouting and cursing carrying into the streets.

Later their names struck me as quaint,
    funny, or absurd:
        Tony's Tap, The Three Musketeers,
           Johnny's Hideaway—
For this is where our people's dream life
    was lived out, where many of the great dramas
    of their lives were enacted—

Or where sorrow met penance
    and came home empty-handed
    and heavy of heart
    with pockets emptied
    to be filled again by life.

MR. B

It didn't bother us when
Mr. Buchaklian became
old and senile and began
drifting up and down
the block, lost but not confused
because he no longer knew
who he was. He didn't need
tending, he never wandered far,
requiring only our sympathy
and tolerance, which we gave,
not knowing that that's
what it was

POOL HALLS
for Chuck Pehlivanian

Smoke-filled, dingy,
suffocating,
with no windows
to let in light
or air
as if our game
were clandestine
vaguely evil
and our presences there
some kind of offense
against ourselves
or something else

And that was how
we felt at times
because even winning
we sensed in the dim light
a falseness,
our money our pores
suffused with dirt
our movements hurried
unalert
with
something
always in fear
of the enclosing
dark

NIGHT

The disturbing cry
of a child
in the night

I would run
from the sound
whenever I heard it
refusing to think whose
child it was
and what made it scream
or cry out loud.
The shades drawn
the light on in a window
high above the ground.

For I had recently
been a child myself
but never screamed
or cried like that
in terror or hurt
nor could I
understand
nor would I ever
find out
how to defend
those that had

KEWPIES

Years before the fast food boom
took over the country
we had such an eatery in Racine
that was known, not for being fast,
but for being good,
and not just because it was convenient,
but for being familiar. And reliable.
The same service. The same food
and atmosphere—every time!

Kewpies sole food, in my mind,
was hamburgers.
They also served pies & cakes
but I can't recall ever having ordered
either of these.
Only hamburgers (usually two)
which were always cooked the same way,
wrapped in the familiar paper covering
with the kewpie doll printed in blue,
and the lettered slogan: *we cater to all the folks*

There was no waiting because the ground beef
was always cooked and ready,
pushed to the back of the flat top burner,
from where it was scooped
into the familiar hamburger bun.
With a pickle placed on top.
Then wrapped and served to its customers.

Most everyone sat at the counter
but there were tables for larger parties.
Root beer was the drink of choice,
and I don't believe anyone tipped,
since the service was minimal,
with the napkin holder on the counter,
the paper wrapper our plate,
and the service so swift,
the eating so quickly accomplished

That you were in and out in an experience
bordering at once on tradition and ritual,
since it seemed to be the one place,
the one event, the one experience,
we all shared in common,
because downtown was where we shopped
and Kewpies was where we ate.

THE LIGHTHOUSE

The lighthouse stood at a safe remove
from the call of the city. A beacon
that lent its strength without needing
to participate in what it beheld.

From the beach and from our lakeshore
drives, we could see it in the distance,
towering, strong, a citadel of pure white
revolving around itself in moving light

Bewitching the waters it looked out upon,
that it no longer protected, but with its
certainty, its surety, and its stability

Giving us that sense of something that was from us
and yet not of us, whose ownership was possessed
by another's hand, and some other mysterious life.

4TH OF JULY

We sat the ancient greens—
the daytime golf links
of Washington Park—
and waited for the fireworks
to start in the night

The moon and the surrounding
constellations looking
down at us from above—
there in the middle of our city,
the park divided by a bridge
the river underneath, that once
carried our Indian name,
soon to reflect the lights
of the fire show about to start

Some mingled, others sat,
all carried by the summer occasion
of a city celebrating its ongoing life

ABOUT THE AUTHOR

David Kherdian was born in Racine, Wisconsin. He is the author and editor
of over fifty books, that include poetry, novels, memoirs, children's books,
as well as critical studies, translations, and retellings. He has published nine
contemporary American poetry anthologies, including his recent BEAT
VOICES (Henry Holt, 1995), and two seminal works: DOWN AT THE SANTA FE
DEPOT: 20 FRESNO POETS (Giligia Press, 1970), that inspired a series of city
and state anthologies, and SETTLING AMERICA: THE ETHNIC EXPRESSION OF
14 CONTEMPORARY AMERICAN POETS (Macmillan, 1974), the first multi-eth-
nic anthology published in this country. Recently, his retelling of MONKEY: A
JOURNEY TO THE WEST (Shambhala, 1992), the most popular classic of Asian
literature, was selected by the Quality Paperback Division of the Book-of-the
Month Club. His numerous awards include a Newbery Honor Book, the
Jane Addams Peace Award, the Friends of American Writers Award, and a
nomination for The American Book Award. He was the editor of *Ararat*
magazine and the founding editor of *Forkroads: A Journal of Ethnic-
American Literature.* He is currently the editor of *Stopinder: A Gurdjieff
Journal for Our Time.* An hour long documentary on his poetry by New York
independent filmmaker Jim Belleau was released in 1997. Shambhala will
publish his life of the Buddha in 2001.

He is married to Caldecott medal winner Nonny Hogrogian and lives in
Oregon.